I CHING

Passages

masculine (he) edition

blended (s/he) edition

split (he/she) edition

twinned (he or she) edition

plural (they) edition

impersonal (one) edition

human (hu) edition

feminine (she) edition

Mudborn Press

I0165115

I Ching—Passages. Copyright © 2014 Mudborn Press
he variant — paper edition ISBN 978-0-930012-28-1

MUDBORN PRESS

NOVELS AND SHORT STORIES

The First Detective, Poe   Hadji Murad, Tolstoy   Goblin Market, Rossetti
Frankenstein & Matilda, Mary Shelley Surfing, Jack London   Ski, Doyle
Martian Testament, The Basement, Eight2Two Benigna Machiavelli, Gilman

INKLINGS & BILINGUAL

Sobre Esta Praia (Sena)   Aztec Birth (Portugés)   At the Fallow's Edge (Ivask)
Italian for Opera Lovers   French for Food Lovers   Yiddish, You Say? Nu?
Mitos y Leyendas/Myths and Legends of Mexico   Berlin: Divided City

SPIRIT

Ghazals of Ghalib   Everlasting Gospel Beechers Thru the 19th Century
The Gospel According to Tolstoy   Gandhi on the Bhagavad Gita

POETRY

Dante & His Circle.   Vita Nuova, Dante   Ovid, The Changes
Aurora Leigh, E.B. Browning Sappho: Poems   Cretan Cycle, Coffey

BANDANNA BOOKS

STAGING SHAKESPEARE

shakespeareplaybook.com DIRECTOR'S PLAYBOOK SERIES

Hamlet   Merchant of Venice Twelfth Night   Taming of the Shrew
A Midsummer Night's Dream Romeo and Juliet As You Like It Richard III
Henry V   Much Ado About Nothing   Macbeth   Othello
  plus   7 Plays with Transgender Characters Falstaff: 4 Plays   Venus and Adonis

TEACHERS SECTION

Don't Panic: Procrastinator's Guide to Term Paper   First Person Intense
SUPPLEMENT EDITIONS
Areopagitica, John Milton   Apology of Socrates, Plato Sappho, The Poems
  Leaves of Grass, Walt Whitman   Uncle Tom's Cabin, Harriet Beecher Stowe
Pi to 500k Decimal Places, Miller   Idea of a President, Madison

INSTRUCTIONS

THE *I CHING* gives advice on how to face any life situation, requiring the seeker to cast yarrowsticks or coins to arrive at an "answer." This edition offers yet another "casting" option, the Button Oracle (online only, at www.bandannabooks.com/iching/button.php); and, if that answer's not enough, use the refresh button. Whether you are a believer or not, the *I Ching*, perhaps the world's oldest book, stands as a remarkable document of human psychology.

However, one translation problem has plagued most Western editions, which typically speak of the "exceptional man" or "he" throughout. To translate assuming that the male pronoun serves for everybody is misleading, however. Why? The language it was written in—Chinese—was, like English, nearly devoid of linguistic gender markers for its pronouns (modern Chinese has added some modifications to clarify gender).

While academics tussle over, or ignore, the "correct third-person-singular-of-unspecified-gender pronoun" for the English language, this Mudborn Press/Bandanna Books edition offers *eight gendered versions* of this text for a modern audience. No, there are not eight genders. But the way that you perceive the human condition may differ from others' views—and your own may change over time.

How to choose? Answer these questions to find the version you are most comfortable with:

Are you all man (using he, him, his), or all woman (she, her, hers)? Or somewhere in between (s/he, him/her, hers/his)? Do you feel like a split personality arguing with yourself (he or she, him or her, his or hers)? — or you feel plural (they, their, theirs)? Or maybe you don't feel strongly one way or the other (asexual: one, one, one's). Or strongly both, as in the shamanic or two-spirit tradition (he-she, her-him, his-hers). Or just as a human (hu, hum, hus). Try more than one version until you reach your comfort zone; you'll learn about yourself as well as about the *I Ching*.

These separate editions are available. You can sample them at www.bandannabooks.com/iching.

I Ching masculine (he)

I Ching feminine (she)

I Ching blended (s/he)

I Ching split (he/she)

I Ching twinned (he or she)

I Ching plural (they)

I Ching impersonal (one)

I Ching human (hu)

This edition is:

I Ching masculine (he)

I CHING   PASSAGES

INTRODUCTION

FOR THIS VERSION of the ancient Chinese oracle, *I Ching: Passages*, I have chosen to present the essential text, figure and lines for each of the 64 hexagrams (6-line figure), plus the commentaries indisputably attributed to Confucius (according to Ku Hsi). Confucius' general comments come at the end of this introduction, but Confucius himself comments on specific hexagrams and lines, as you will find in the text.

Many commentaries on the *I Ching* have been written since King Wen and his son the Duke of Chou, purported authors of the original text, themselves wrote commentaries for it. For a taste of commentaries written in different eras, consult the Wilhelm/Baynes retranslation, the oft-reprinted nineteenth-century version by James Legge, and John Blofeld's 1965 edition. Many recent translations emphasize new-ageism, feminism, etc. This edition of the translation is one of eight in a series of gender variant versions.

The symbolism of a hexagram is based on the essential dualism of Chinese thinking—the yin and the yang, weak and strong, dark and light, man and woman, earth and heaven. Thus each line of a hexagram is either solid (yang) or broken (yin), and, because a hexagram has six lines, there are only 64 possible hexagrams. Each hexagram may be thought of as two trigrams; there are only 8 possible trigrams, and each combination of two trigrams is spelled out in each Figure section, as, for example, lake atop mountain, or chasm within chasm. Since the whole universe of possibilities must be included in these 64 hexagrams, the oracle may be said to answer to any situation.

The answers one finds in the *I Ching* give the relations between people, within a family, or in a state. Though quaint images may be used, the center of concern in the *I Ching* is always ethics and morality, the behavior of human beings. For this reason, Confucius greatly favored its use as a great humanist document. No matter what "fortune" a man may find in it, he learns something essential about the human condition, and, like the answers of the Delphic Oracle in Greece, the answers may have to wait a long time for the right questions to be asked.

The Master says: What is it that the Passages do?

The Passages disclose natural things, perfect affairs of humans, and encompass all things on earth—this and nothing else the Passages accomplish. By means of the Book, the sages set a proper direction to every purpose, give evenness to every field of action, and settle all doubts.

The Master says: Writing doesn't fully express speech, and speech doesn't completely express ideas. Is it impossible to determine the ideas of the sages?

The sages invented ideograms to express their thoughts fully; they organized the hexagrams to express true and false completely. Then they added explanations and the movable lines to express their words adequately. They enlivened it all with drums and dancing, thus completely developing the spirit of the *I Ching*.

The Master says: In the whole of nature, what part is thinking? what part planning?

Everything returns at last to the same end, though they come by different paths. There is one result for all the hopes of a hundred schemes. In nature, what is thinking? what is planning?

The Master says: The Creative and the Receptive are really the
gate to the Passages. The Creative represents bright active things
and the Receptive dark inactive things. As the dark and light
join, various positions for the firm and yielding lines embody
the hexagrams. Thus heaven and earth are made visible, and
we can grasp the inner workings of the intelligence of spirit.

The Master says: Whoever knows the schema of the changes, passages,
and transformations knows what is done by that spiritual power.

CONSULTING THE COIN ORACLE

BEFORE YOU TOSS coins or cast sticks, let your mind clear of extraneous matters. You are about to consult the Oracle on a matter of great concern to you. A question need not be specific—you are at a crossroads in your life, and you seek advice about which path to take. Or you are in some difficulty and don't see any easy way out. Meditate on your concern, and try to put it into words so that the Oracle may clarify it for you. Breathe. Now you are ready.

COIN ORACLE: The coin oracle is accomplished by 6 tosses of 3 coins. Any coins will do, but if you can, use old Chinese bronze coins, usually inscribed on one side with a hole in the middle. The inscribed side, or "heads," showing on a coin gives a value of 2; the blank side, or "tails," gives 3. Therefore, any toss of three coins will result in values totaling 6, 7, 8, or 9.

   ◇ 6: A sum of 6 (all heads) gives you old yin (a "moving" line); draw a line with two parts separated by a small X at its middle. –x–

   ◇ 7: A sum of 7 (two heads & a tails) gives young yang (a "nonmoving" line); draw a solid line. ——

   ◇ 8: A sum of 8 (two tails & a heads) is young yin (nonmoving); draw a line with two parts.— —

   ◇ 9: A sum of 9 (all tails) is old yang (moving); draw a solid line with a little circle in its middle. –o–

    Lines of the hexagram are drawn beginning at the bottom, so that the top line is the sixth and last. For your first line, calculate the sum value from your first throw, using the table above, and draw your first line. Now cast the coins five more times, repeating the steps above, until you have a hexagram (6 lines) drawn.

Now, if you have any moving lines in your hexagram, you will draw a second hexagram beside the first, repeating with no change all the nonmoving lines, but wherever the first hexagram has a moving line, you draw its opposite in the corresponding position in the second hexagram. If your moving line is old yang (–o–), the new line is young yin (— —), and if your moving line is old yin (–x–), you now draw young yang (——). In the exceptional case where you have no moving lines at all, then you are assured that your answer is pretty much on target already, and no second hexagram is needed.

Now you consult the table to find your oracle: look up the first hexagram, and read the Text and the Figure. Then in Lines, you read only where you have a moving line. Pay particular attention to the message of any moving line marked by a little circle; this is a ruling line in its hexagram, and its meaning may have additional significance. As a final step, look up the second hexagram and read Text and Figure. And that's your answer.

YARROWSTICK ORACLE

Take 50 sticks, remove 1 and don't use it again. Divide
the rest into two piles. Take 1 from the right pile and put
it in a discard pile. Now, discard 4 sticks at a time from
the left pile until there are 4 or fewer left in the pile. Do
the same with the righthand pile. When this is done, you
will have a total in both piles of either 8 or 4 sticks. 4 is
yang, and gets a value of 3; 8 is yin, and is valued at 2.
Remember this value. Now you put aside the 8 or 4, pick
up all the sticks from the discard pile, and divide these
into two piles. Just as before, you discard one from the
right pile, take away sticks 4 at a time from the left pile,
then from the right. Now calculate your sum, this time
including the first discarded stick, and you should have 8
or 4 (valued at 2 or 3). Repeat this procedure a third time,
so that now you have three values (of either 2 or 3), which
you now total. You will now have a figure of 6, 7, 8, or 9
and you can now draw your first line. Consult the table
in the Coin Oracle for instructions on drawing lines.

For the next line, gather all 50 stalks together
and begin again. When you have completed this
six times, you should have your hexagram. Follow
directions in the last two paragraphs of the Coin
Oracle. And finally, consult the table of trigrams on
the next page to locate your reading in the I Ching.

TABLE OF SIGNS

lower trigram ↓	upper trigram							
	Ch'ien	Tui	Li	Sun	Chen	K'an	Ken	Kun
Ch'ien	1	43	14	9	34	5	26	11
Tui	10	58	38	61	54	60	41	19
Li	13	49	30	37	55	63	22	36
Sun	44	28	50	57	32	48	18	46
Chen	25	17	21	42	51	3	27	24
K'an	6	47	64	59	40	29	4	7
Ken	33	31	56	53	62	39	52	15
Kun	12	45	35	20	16	8	23	2

A REMINDER: This "HE" version uses the traditional or old-fashioned "universal he" pronoun for third-person human reference where sex is not specified, or not known. The *I Ching* frequently speaks of a hypothetical person, the exceptional or uncommon person; it is used here quite often.

14

I CHING : the Text

CH'IEN
1. THE CREATIVE

TEXT: The Creative. Great success. Persistence on a moral path is rewarded.

FIGURE: Powerful forces are moving in the sky. The exceptional man works constantly to strengthen his character.

◇ LINES: 1. (9 at the bottom) Thunder dragon is hiding. Don't act.

• *The Master says*: He has a dragon's power, yet he lies hidden. The world little influences him; he does nothing to make a name for himself. He is not sad at withdrawing from the world. He weathers disapproval without sadness. In happy times, he follows his principles; in sad times, he retires them. Indeed, he can't be uprooted; he is the hidden dragon.

◇2. (9) Dragon appears in an open field. To meet a great man is favorable.

• *The Master says*: He has the dragon's power, and holds the center. In ordinary speech he is reliable; in ordinary actions he is earnest. He guards against vice and preserves his integrity. his goodness is known, but he doesn't boast. By his character, he influences people and transforms them.

◇ 3. (9) All day long the excellent man is busy. At night he is wide awake. Danger. No mistake.

• *The Master says*: The uncommon man improves

his character and practices all his skills. Through loyalty and faith he improves his character. He pays attention to his words, so that they are firmly based on truth, and his work will endure. He knows how to achieve this, and he achieves it; he is in accord with the origin of things. He knows how to bring it to a good end, and does so; he makes it truly enduring. Thus he occupies a high position without pride or a low one without disappointment. He is active yet careful, so that even in danger he makes no mistake.

◇ 4. (9) Hopping around at the brink of a chasm. No error.

* *The Master says*: He finds no permanent place either high or low, so he doesn't go ahead. Advancing or retreating are equal to him, since he has no place of his own; but he doesn't leave his friends. The uncommon man builds his character and practices his skills, so that he may do everything at the right time; thus he makes no mistake.

◇ ◇ 5. (9) Dragon winging through the sky. To visit a great man is advantageous.

• *The Master says*: Notes in the same chord vibrate together. Animals of the same nature seek out each other. Water flows toward the low, fire seeks what is dry. Clouds follow the dragon, wind follows the tiger. The sage appears, and all humans look up to him. Those born of heaven are drawn to what is above. Those born of earth stick to what is below. Each follows its own kind.

◇ 6. (9 at the top) An arrogant dragon. Cause for sorrow.

• *The Master says*: He is noble but has no suitable office; he stands high but no one acknowledges him; he has an able assistant who doesn't support him. He will meet grief at every turn.

◇ 7. (all 9s) A gaggle of dragons losing their heads. Good luck.

K'UN
2. THE RECEPTIVE

TEXT: The Receptive means great success, as seen in the steadiness of a mare. If the exceptional man must move, and tries to lead, he goes astray; but if he follows, he finds his way. The advantage is in finding friends in the southwest, and losing friends in the northeast. Orderly and firm persistence brings good fortune.

FIGURE: The powers of earth forces act by receptivity. The uncommon man of highest character embraces the whole world.

⟨⟩ LINES: 1. (6 at the bottom) Walking on hoarfrost. Solid ice will come soon.

⟨⟩ 2. (6) Straight, square, and capacious. Though without effort, everything prospers.

⟨⟩ 3. (6) Keeping talents firmly hidden is the proper course. In public service, though success may not be claimed, yet one can bring affairs to completion.

⟨⟩ 4. (6) A tied sack. No reason to blame or to praise.

⟨⟩ 5. (6) Yellow clothing. Great good fortune.

⟨⟩ 6. (6) Dragons fight in the backcountry. Their blood is blue-black and yellow.

⟨⟩ 7. (all 6s) Unvarying determination presses the advantage.

CHUN
3. OBSTACLE

TEXT: After an initial obstacle, great progress. Steady effort is rewarded, but nothing should be started now. One should consolidate gains by appointing lieutenants.

FIGURE: Clouds release lightning and thunder. The uncommon man is occupied in creating order.

◇ LINES: ◇ 1. (9 at the bottom) Hindrance to movement. One should keep still and steady. Advantage comes with position.

◇ 2. (6) Obstacles pile up, forcing a return, even by a horse-drawn carriage. He is not a rapist, he seeks the young woman's hand in marriage. She remains a virgin, and turns him down. After ten years, she will take marriage vows.

◇ 3. (6) Following deer without a woodsman, one gets lost in the forest. The uncommon man, sensing hidden danger, forsakes the hunt. To persist brings trouble.

◇ 4. (6) Her horse-drawn wagon withdraws. She asks help of her suitor. To go ahead brings good fortune. Everything undertaken turns out well.

◇ ◇ 5. (9) Obstacles to getting an expected blessing. Steadiness in small matters brings good fortune. Persistence in great issues creates disaster.

◇ 6. (6 at the top) His horses in harness are forced back. Blood and tears flow.

MENG
4. CHILDISHNESS

TEXT: Childishness. Success. I'm not looking for the raw youth, the youth seeks me out. The first time he consults the oracle, I answer. To ask a second or third time is to nag, and I don't respond to a nag. Stability improves matters.

FIGURE: A pond at the foot of a mountain. The exceptional man builds character by taking care of detail in everything.

‹› LINES: 1. (6 at the bottom) To foster maturity, discipline is required. Even restraints may be used, but to continue to use them is harmful.

‹› ‹› 2. (9) Gentleness in dealing with fools brings good fortune. Knowing how to appreciate women also is fortunate. The son can handle household affairs.

‹› 3. (6) Don't marry a woman who loses her head when she sees a wealthy man. No advantage can be gained.

‹› 4. (6) Perplexed inexperience brings embarrassment.

‹› ‹› 5. (6) Naive innocence produces good fortune.

‹› 6. (9 at the top) In disciplining the immature, one should not wrong him. The only advantage is in preventing harm to him.

Hsu
5. Postponement

TEXT: Genuine restraint wins brilliant success. Persistence allows good fortune. It is advantageous to cross the big water.

FIGURE: Clouds rise to the highest point. The uncommon man bides his time eating, drinking with delight.

⟨⟩ LINES: 1. (9 at the bottom) Patient waiting on the outskirts prevents harm. No mistake.

⟨⟩ 2. (9) Waiting in the river sand. A little gossip, but at last everything will turn out fine.

⟨⟩ 3. (9) Staying in the mud allows harm to approach.

⟨⟩ 4. (6) Inactivity amid blood. Get out of the cave.

⟨⟩ ⟨⟩ 5. (9) Staying in the midst of meat and drink. Steadiness brings good fortune.

⟨⟩ 6. (6 at the top) Entering the cave. Three uninvited guests arrive. Respect for them will bring good fortune at last.

SUNG
6. CONFLICT

TEXT: Conflict. Despite sincerity, one is being obstructed. Guarded caution up to the middle is rewarded, but to go on to the end is disastrous. A man gains by visiting the great human, but not by crossing the big river.

FIGURE: Sky and water are opposed. Before undertaking any action, the exceptional man carefully plans its beginning.

◇ LINES: 1. (6 at the bottom) One shouldn't sustain the affair. A little gossip does not prevent good fortune in the end.

◇ 2. (9) The conflict can't be resolved; he gives up. If he hides at home among the 300 families of his clan, he escapes harm.

◇ 3. (6) Remaining firmly in the old assigned position is dangerous. In the end, good fortune. If you happen to be in public service, don't expect to achieve.

◇ 4. (9) One cannot win the conflict. He resigns himself to fate and changes his policy. Peaceful persistence brings good fortune.

◇ ◇ 5. (9) Contention brings great good fortune.

◇ 6. (9 at the top) If a man were to be honored with a leather belt, it would be taken away three times that same morning.

SHIH
7. THE ARMY

TEXT: The Army. Strong and experienced leaders persevering in goodness bring good fortune and no error.

FIGURE: Water surrounded by land. The uncommon man cultivates his people, and acts generously toward them.

◇ LINES: 1. (6 at the bottom) An army is built on discipline. Without order, catastrophe threatens.

◇ ◇ 2. (9) The leader in the midst of the army has good fortune and no error. Three times he is honored by the king.

◇ 3. (6) The army carries deadwood in the wagons. Tragedy.

◇ 4. (6) The army retreats. No fault.

◇ ◇ 5. (6) Wild animals in the field; one may catch some with no blame. If the oldest son leads the army while younger sons cart awa corpses, then persistence in this arrangement will bring disaster.

◇ 6. (6 at the top) A great prince is given a mandate; he founds states and appoints clan chiefs. Incompetent people should not be used.

Pɪ
8. Association

TEXT: Harmonization brings good fortune. Ask the oracle once more whether or not you are great, steadfast, and firm. If so, then there is no error. Those who are doubtful come together, but those who come late face disaster.

FIGURE: Water on the land. Long ago the rulers assigned various states to feudal lords and kept on friendly terms with them.

‹› LINES: 1. (6 at the bottom) His sincerity wins a loyal following, with no mistake. Trust may accumulate to overflowing, as in an earthenware bowl, and good fortune will come from elsewhere.
   ‹› 2. (6) Cooperation comes from the inside. Steadiness brings good fortune.
   ‹› 3. (6) Association with the wrong people.
   ‹› 4. (6) Cooperation with someone beyond one's circle. Persistence is rewarded.
   ‹› ‹› 5. (9) An instance of coordination: the king pursues game on three sides, but the quarry escapes by running ahead. The people are not warned in advance. Good fortune.
   ‹› 6. (6 at the top) To seek unification without a leader ends in disaster.

HSIAO CHU
9. THE LITTLE CULTIVATOR

TEXT: The Little Cultivator has success. Dense clouds that do not rain come from the western border.

FIGURE: Wind blows across the sky. The uncommon man shows the grace of his character.

‹› LINES: 1. (9 at the bottom) He returns to his path; how could one blame him? Good fortune.

‹› 2. (9) He lets himself be drawn back into old ways. Good fortune.

‹› 3. (9) The carriage wheels break off from the wagon. Husband and wife avoid each other's eyes.

‹› 4. (6) With sincerity, bloodshed is avoided and fear vanishes. No error.

‹› ‹› 5. (9) Confidence draws others to join. One's neighbors are enriched.

‹› 6. (9 at the top) Rain falls, and rest comes. Character endures and builds. Persistence brings danger to the woman. The moon is nearly full. If the exceptional man proceeds now, misfortune will come.

Lu
10. TREADING

TEXT: Treading on the tiger's tail. It doesn't bite the man. Success.

FIGURE: A lake open to the sky. The uncommon man distinguishes high from low, thus strengthening the people's self-control.

‹› LINES: 1. (9 at the bottom) Walking forward on the usual path is blameless.

‹› 2. (9) A lone walker striding steadily on an easy level path. Good fortune.

‹› 3. (6) A one-eyed man can still see, a lame man can walk. He steps on the tiger's tail. The tiger bites him. Bad luck. A soldier acts as agent for his ruler.

‹› 4. (9) Walking on the tail of the tiger with prudence and discretion leads at last to good fortune.

‹› ‹› 5. (9) Walking firmly. Persistence gives rise to danger.

‹› 6. (9 at the top) Watch your step and consider the signs. If they measure up, great good fortune comes.

T'AI
11. PEACE

TEXT: Peace. The second-rate departs, the great comes near. Good fortune and success.

FIGURE: Sky and earth come together. The great ruler by perceptive regulation of matters fulfills the destinies of heaven and earth; people everywhere are comforted.

⟨⟩ LINES: 1. (9 at the bottom) When grass is pulled up, other roots come too. Continuations bring good fortune.

⟨⟩ ⟨⟩ 2. (9) He is respectful even to the unschooled, can cross the river without a boat, does not neglect distant friends, does not take friends for granted. In such ways he manages to walk the middle path.

⟨⟩ 3. (9) A plain is followed by a slope. Leaving is followed by a return. Stubbornness in the face of danger is not a mistake. Don't be sad; enjoy the happiness you already have.

⟨⟩ 4. (6) Fluttering about, he doesn't boast of wealth to his neighbor; he is artless and sincere.

⟨⟩ ⟨⟩ 5. (6) The emperor gives his daughter in marriage. Happiness and great good fortune.

⟨⟩ 6. (6 at the top) The wall has fallen into the moat. Don't use the army now. Lay down your rules in your own town. Perseverance will bring blame.

P'I
12. STAGNATION

TEXT: Stagnation. The steadiness of the exceptional man is obstructed by lack of good will among people. The great are gone; the mediocre come near.

FIGURE: Sky and earth don't meet. The exceptional man retreats into his inner self to avoid bad influences. He isn't tempted by honors or cash.

◇ 1. (6 at the bottom) When grass is pulled up, other roots come too. Steadiness brings good fortune and success.

◇ 2. (6) Patience and endurance in underlings means good fortune. The great man grapples with stagnation and gains success.

◇ 3. (6) He is ashamed of his hidden purpose.

◇ 4. (9) Obedience to the highest command is never wrong. One's companions share in this blessing.

◇ ◇ 5. (9) Stagnation is lessening. Fortune favors the great man. If thoughts of failure come, one must firm things up, like mulberry branches tied together to shape a bush.

• *The Master says*: Keeping danger in mind makes a man secure in his position. Keeping the threat of destruction in mind, a man better preserves his estate. Keeping the possibility of confusion in mind allows a man to put everything in order. Therefore the uncommon man does not forget danger when secure, nor ruin when well established, nor disorder when everything is tidy. These habits enhance his personal safety and he is able to protect the provinces and the clans.

◇ 6. (9 at the top) The obstruction is overcome. At first stagnation, and now great joy.

T'UNG JEN
13. FELLOWSHIP

TEXT: Fellowship in public. Success. Crossing the big water is favorable. Steadiness in the exceptional man is advantageous.

FIGURE: Sky together with fire. The exceptional man handles every affair in a manner appropriate to it.

⟨⟩ LINES: 1. (9 at the bottom) A friend at the gate. No mistake.

⟨⟩ ⟨⟩ 2. (6) Fellowship within the clan. Trouble.

⟨⟩ 3. (9) He hides his weapons in the thicket, and climbs a high hill. For three years he shows no sign.

⟨⟩ 4. (9) He climbs the city wall; he can't attack. Good fortune.

⟨⟩ ⟨⟩ 5. (9) Friends at first cry and moan, but later they laugh. Struggling through a mob, they succeed in coming together.

• *The Master says*: The lives of good persons run on different paths.

> One works as a public official;
> another at home fills his time in arts.
> One man knows but does not say,
> while another expresses everything he thinks.
> But when two are as one in their hearts,
> Iron locks will not keep them apart;

The words they use in their oneness
permeate the air like the fragrance of orchids.

◇ 6. (9 at the top) Fellowship at the outskirts. No cause
for regret.

TA YU
14. WEALTH

TEXT: Wealth brings great success.

FIGURE: Fire in the sky. The exceptional man suppresses evil and protects good people. Gladly he obeys the will of heaven.

‹› LINES: 1. (9 at the bottom): He has nothing to do with evil and is blameless. As long as he is aware of problems, he isn't in error.

‹› 2. (9) A big supply wagon. One may go in any direction and not be in error.

‹› 3. (9) A prince may present offerings to the emperor. An ordinary man can't do this.

‹› 4. (9) He holds back his resources. No blame.

‹› ‹› 5. (6) His sincerity makes him open to all. Dignity brings good fortune.

‹› 6. (9 at the top) Those who are helped by heaven have good fortune and success in everything.

CH'IEN
15. MODESTY

TEXT: Modesty brings success. The uncommon man carries matters through to completion.

FIGURE: A mountain inside the earth. The uncommon man takes away from what has too much, and gives to what has too little. He weighs things and equalizes them.

⟨⟩ LINES: 1. (6 at the bottom) An exceptional man exceptionally modest may cross the big water. Good fortune.

⟨⟩ 2. (6) Humility that is recognized. Earnestness brings good fortune.

⟨⟩ ⟨⟩ 3. (9) An uncommon man of merit modestly brings matters to completion. Good fortune.

• *The Master says*: When a man puts forth great effort without boasting, and doesn't consider his rewards a virtue, he is a man of great generosity. For all his great merit, he places others before himself. He strives to perfect his virtue, he is always respectful to others. The modest man through respectfulness will be able to maintain his position.

⟨⟩ 4. (6) Everything is favorable when the modest man is moved to action.

⟨⟩ 5. (6) Modesty about wealth in front of neighbors. To attack now is favorable in every way.

⟨⟩ 6. (6 at the top) Humility that is recognized. One may favorably set armies marching, but only to subdue one's own city and country.

Yu
16. COMPLACENCY

TEXT: Complacency is favorable for appointing princes and setting armies in motion.

FIGURE: Thunder over the earth. The ancient rulers honored merit in song, and made grand sacrifices to Heaven to honor their ancestors.

‹› LINES: 1. (6 at the bottom) For a cock to crow complacently brings misfortune.

‹› 2. (6) Firm as a rock. Before a day passes, persistence brings good fortune.

• *The Master says*: To know the origins of things is spiritual wisdom. When associating with higher-ups, the uncommon man doesn't flatter. When interacting with underlings, he isn't coarse. He knows the seeds. The seeds are the first slight beginning of movement, the earliest trace of destiny, be it good or bad. The uncommon man watches them and immediately takes appropriate action; he doesn't wait even a single day.

o Firm as a rock, why should he wait a whole day; he already knows. The uncommon man knows the subtle and the obvious. He knows weak from strong. Ten thousand look up to him.

‹› 3. (6) Looking up complacently brings regret. Hesitation brings sorrow.

◇ ◇ 4. (9) Out of self-satisfaction, he achieves great success. Don't doubt it; friends gather around you like hair gathered in a ribbon.

◇ 5. (6) Chronic illness, but not death.

◇ 6. (6 at the top) Unthinking smugness. Even if a man goes through to the end before changing his attitude, he is not blamed.

Sui
17. Following

TEXT: Following has great success. Steadiness is rewarded. No mistake.

FIGURE: Thunder in the middle of a swamp. At night the exceptional man goes indoors for peace and rest.

‹› LINES: *1. (9 at the bottom) The leadership is changing. Steadiness brings good fortune. To go out and mingle with people produces results.

‹› 2. (6) He clings to the child, and loses the man of character.

‹› 3. (6) He clings to the adult, and loses the child. By following, one finds what one needs. Better is to stay on the course of goodness.

‹› 4. (9) He gains followers successfully, but to go on in this way will bring misfortune. Proceeding with sincerity brings clarity; how could he make a mistake?

‹› ‹› 5. (9) Trustworthiness breeds excellence. Good fortune.

‹› 6. (6 at the top) He gains firm loyalty from his followers, and further binds them to himself. The ruler sacrifices to his ancestors at the Western Mountain.

Ku
18. DECAY

TEXT: Decay has great success. Crossing the big water is profitable. Three days before the start, three days after the start.

FIGURE: Wind blows low on the mountain. The uncommon man invigorates the people and fosters their goodness

◇ LINES: 1. (6 at the bottom) A son correcting the problems created by the father; if he succeeds, the dead father is freed from blame. Danger, but good fortune in the end.

◇ 2. (9) In setting right the errors of the mother, one shouldn't be too stubborn.

◇ 3. (9) To correct the troubles caused by the father will bring a little remorse, but not much blame.

◇ 4. (6) Tolerating the errors of the father eventually brings regret.

◇ ◇ 5. (6) Taking on the task of rectifying problems created by the father is praiseworthy.

◇ 6. (9 at the top) He doesn't serve king or prince; he sets his own higher goals.

19. APPROACH

TEXT: Approach has great success. Steadiness is advantageous. In the eighth month, misfortune.

FIGURE: Land rising out of a lake. The exceptional man has boundless affection and eagerness to teach. There is no limit in his caring for the people.

‹› LINES: *1. (9 at the bottom) Convergence. Earnestness brings good fortune.

‹› ‹› 2. (9) Convergence. Good fortune. Everything is favorable.

‹› 3. (6) An easy approach, but with no advantage. If one regrets it, he is not in error.

‹› 4. (6) A perfect approach. No mistake.

‹› 5. (6) Wisdom approaches, suitable for a great prince. Good fortune.

‹› 6. (6 at the top) Generosity approaches. Good fortune. No error.

KUAN
20. VIEWING

TEXT: Viewing. He has washed his hands, but hasn't made the offering yet. His sincerity gains respect.

FIGURE: Wind blows across the earth. The old rulers visited the various regions to observe their people and teach them.

◇ LINES: 1. (6 at the bottom) An adolescent stares—not a mistake in an ordinary man, but for an exceptional man, humiliation.

◇ 2. (6) Watching through a door open just a crack. For a woman, persistence is profitable.

◇ 3. (6) We examine our own life and then we advance or retreat.

◇ 4. (6) Viewing the brilliance of the nation. The advantage is in being a guest of the ruler.

◇ ◇ 5. (9) When the uncommon man examines his own life, no mistake is made.

◇ ◇ 6. (9 at the top) Looking at one's own life to see if one is exceptional is blameless.

SHIH HO
21. CHEWING

TEXT: Chewing has success. One gains by resorting to legal recourse.

FIGURE: Thunder and lightning. The old rulers clearly defined a legal code and enforced it resolutely.

‹› LINES: 1. (9 at the bottom) His feet are in the stocks, and his toes are bitten off. No error.

• *The Master says:* A mediocre man isn't ashamed of being unkind nor does he shrink from doing evil. Where he sees no advantage, he makes no effort to be good; if he isn't threatened, he wouldn't change. But, fortunately for the mediocre man, if he corrects himself in small ways, he can be careful in large ones.

‹› 2. (6) Chews tender flesh, and his nose is bitten off. No blame.

‹› 3. (6) Chews on dried meat and bites something disagreeable. Slight illness, but no fault.

‹› 4. (9) Chews meat dried on the bone, and finds a metal arrow. One should pay attention to problems and to be steadfast. Good fortune.

‹› ‹› 5. (6) Chews dried meat and finds gold. Constant vigil brings danger, but no mistake.

‹› 6. (9 at the top) His neck is locked in a wooden yoke, and his ears are bitten off. Misfortune.

22. Sᴛʏʟᴇ

TEXT: Style has success. Small advantages may be gained by pursuing a goal.

FIGURE: Fire at the foot of a mountain. The uncommon man takes care of the present situation, but he dare not settle legal controversies.

◇ LINES: 1. (9 at the bottom) In stylish shoes, he leaves the car behind and walks.

◇ ◇ 2. (6) He styles his face whiskers.

◇ 3. (9) Graceful and glistening. Continual steadiness brings good fortune.

◇ 4. (6) Dressed tastefully in white, he comes on a winged white horse. He steps in, not to plunder but to propose.

◇ 5. (6) He strolls gracefully in the hills and gardens. The bolt of silk is small and cheap. Disgrace, but in the end good fortune.

◇ ◇ 6. (9 at the top) To dress plainly is not a mistake.

Po
23. Shedding

TEXT: Shedding. There's no advantage in going anywhere.

FIGURE: A mountain rests on the earth. Those in the leadership give generously to their juniors to ensure comfort and peace.

◇ LINES: 1. (6 at the bottom) The leg of the bed is broken off, and steadiness is impossible. Misfortune.

◇ 2. (6) The frame of the bed is split. Steadiness is gone. Misfortune.

◇ 3. (6) He separates from all of them, with no guilt.

◇ 4. (6) The bed splits right through the mattress. Misfortune.

◇ 5. (6) A string of fish. Good fortune comes by the endorsement of the ladies at court. Everything is favorable.

◇ ◇ 6. (9 at the top) A ripe fruit is uneaten. The exceptional man gains a car. The ordinary man loses his house.

Fu
24. Return

TEXT: Return means success. No one prevents him going or coming. Friends come, no error. He returns to his normal course within seven days. Wherever he goes, he gains.

FIGURE: Thunder in the earth. The old rulers closed the passes during the solstice festivals. Merchants couldn't travel, even the ruler didn't tour the provinces.

⟨⟩ LINES *1. (9 at the bottom) A quick roundtrip, with nothing to regret. Great good fortune.

• *The Master says*: Yen Hui nearly attained perfection. If he had a fault, he was sure to recognize it; once he recognized it, he never made the same mistake again.

⟨⟩ 2. (6) A worthy return. Good fortune.

⟨⟩ 3. (6) Repeated returns mean trouble, but not a mistake.

⟨⟩ 4. (6) He walks in the middle of a crowd, yet he returns alone.

⟨⟩ 5. (6) An honorable return, no regret.

⟨⟩ 6. (6 at the top) To return in disarray means misfortune, with calamities and bodily injury. If armies are ordered forth like this, one at last suffers a great defeat, affecting even the nation's ruler. Even ten years will not suffice to set things right again.

Wu Wang
25. Honesty

TEXT: Honesty means great success. Steadiness is rewarded. If one isn't upright, he has misfortune; there's no point in undertaking anything.

FIGURE: Thunder rolls across the sky, quickening the growth of all things. The old rulers, in harmony with the seasons, fed everyone abundantly.

‹› LINES: *1. (9 at the bottom) Proceeding with sincerity brings good fortune.

‹› 2. (6) One shouldn't calculate the harvest while plowing the ground for it, nor reap the third year's crop while planting the first year's seeds. One gains by setting a goal.

‹› 3. (6) Unexpected misfortune. A cow is roped and led away; the passer-by's gain is the farmer's loss.

‹› 4. (9) Stubborn uprightness is blameless.

‹› ‹› 5. (9) The honest man falls ill. Don't treat it with medicines, it will pass.

‹› 6. (9 at the top) An honest action brings misfortune. One only gains by doing nothing.

Ta Ch'u
26. The Big Cultivator

TEXT: The Big Cultivator brings steadiness. Not eating at home results in good fortune. Crossing the big water is profitable.

FIGURE: The sky among the mountains. The exceptional man becomes familiar with the sayings and deeds of wise men of the past, and so invigorates his character.

‹› LINES: 1. (9 at the bottom) Danger is close. Best to stop one's course of action.

‹› 2. (9) The wagon's axles are removed.

‹› 3. (9) A good horse urged to a gallop. Once the danger is understood, steadiness and daily practice in chariots and defensive techniques help. Then, wherever one goes, one gains.

‹› 4. (6) The hornguards of a young bull. Great good fortune.

‹› ‹› 5. (6) The tusks of a gelded boar. Good fortune.

‹› ‹› 6. (9 at the top) The agent of the way of heaven. Success.

I
27. JAWS

TEXT: Jaws. Steadiness brings good fortune. Pay attention to nourishment and observe the food that a man seeks.

FIGURE: Thunder rumbles at the foot of a mountain. The uncommon man speaks carefully and eats and drinks moderately.

◇ LINES: 1. (9 at the bottom) You release your precious tortoise, and stare at me with your mouth open. Misfortune.

◇ 2. (6) Nourishment on the mountain peak; turning away, he seeks sustenance in the hills, which leads to misfortune.

◇ 3. (6) He rejects nourishment. To keep fasting will bring misfortune. For ten years he does nothing useful, and there is nowhere to go.

◇ 4. (6) Nourishment on the mountaintop brings good fortune. His eyes gleam like a hungry tiger's as he is about to pounce. No fault.

◇ ◇ 5. (6) One turns away from the usual path. Steadfastness brings good fortune. One should not cross the big water.

◇ ◇ 6. (9 at the top) Nourishment gives rise to danger, but also brings good fortune. Crossing the big water is fruitful.

TEXT: Excess. The ridgepole bends. One may move in any direction advantageously. Success.

FIGURE: A forest swamped by water. The exceptional man, though standing alone, has no fear; he is not perturbed when withdrawing from the world.

◇ LINES: 1. (6 at the bottom) Mats of white rush-grass placed on the ground for protection are no mistake.

• *The Master says*: Simply putting something on the floor is sufficient. But when he puts white rushes underneath them, how could that be a mistake? This is being extremely cautious. The reeds themselves have no value, but their effect can be very important. If he is as careful in everything he does, no mistake will be made.

◇ ◇ 2. (9) A dead willow sends up new sprouts around the root. An old man marries a young wife. Everything is favorable.

◇ 3. (9) The ridgepole weakens. Misfortune.

◇ ◇ 4. (9) The ridgepole is buttressed. Good fortune. Any other course brings regret.

◇ 5. (9) A decayed willow blossoms. An old woman marries a young husband. Neither blame nor praise.

◇ 6. (6 at the top) While fording the river, water comes up over one's head. Misfortune, but no fault.

K'AN
29. CHASM

TEXT: Chasm inside chasm. If you are honest and keep your wits sharp, whatever you do will succeed.

FIGURE: Water flows on uninterruptedly. The exceptional man lives by imperishable truths and never ceases teaching.

‹› LINES: 1. (6 at the bottom) Chasm inside chasm. In one ravine, he falls into a cave. Misfortune.

‹› ‹› 2. (9) The chasm is dangerous. One achieves only small goals.

‹› 3. (6) Coming or going, one faces a dangerous chasm. He descends into a cavern. There is nothing to do.

‹› 4. (6) A bottle of wine, an extra bowl of rice; earthenware handed in through a window. Ultimately there is no blame.

‹› ‹› 5. (9) Water in the chasm has not risen to overflowing, yet it maintains a high level. No fault.

‹› 6. (6 at the top) Tied up by rope, hemmed in by thorns. For three years he can't find his way. Misfortune.

Li
30. Brilliance

TEXT: Brilliance. Steadiness brings reward. Success. Tending cattle brings good fortune.

FIGURE: Twin tongues of flame. The exceptional man, by keeping alive intelligence, lights up every part of the world.

◇ LINES: 1. (9 at the bottom) He walks erratically, but if he is reverent, there is no fault.

◇ ◇ 2. (6) Yellow light. Great good fortune.

◇ 3. (9) In the light of the setting sun, instead of beating the earthenware drum and singing, he loudly bemoans his approaching old age. Misfortune.

◇ 4. (9) It comes suddenly; abruptly it flares up, then dies, and is tossed out.

◇ ◇ 5. (6) A flood of tears, sighing and sorrowing. Good fortune.

◇ 6. (9 at the top) The ruler sends him marching forth to quell a rebellion. He kills the leaders, but doesn't punish the followers. No mistake.

HSIEN
31. FEELING

TEXT: Feeling means success. Steadiness is rewarded. Marrying a young wife brings good fortune.

FIGURE: A mountain lake. The uncommon man is available to everyone equally.

◇ LINES: 1. (6 at the bottom) Feeling in the big toe.

◇ 2. (6) Feeling in the calves of the legs. Misfortune. Staying put brings good fortune.

◇ 3. (9) Feeling in the thighs. He clings to followers, but to continue to do so will be regretted.

◇ ◇ 4. (9) Persistence brings good fortune, with no need to apologize. If a man's mind leaps about from one idea to another, only his friends will understand his purpose.

• *The Master says:* What need has nature of thought and care? In nature all things return to their common source and are distributed along different paths; through one action, the fruits of a hundred thoughts are realized. What need has nature of thought, of care?

◇ ◇ 5. (9) Feeling in the skin along the spine. No regret.

◇ 6. (6 at the top) Feeling in the jaws and tongue.

32. CONSTANCY

TEXT: Constancy has success. No fault. Steadiness brings gain. Going anywhere is advantageous.

FIGURE: Thunder with wind. The uncommon man stands firm and can't be moved.

‹› LINES: 1. (6 at the bottom) He desires to last, but simple persistence creates misfortune. No advantage is gained.

‹› ‹› 2. (9) Sorrow vanishes.

‹› 3. (9) His character has no staying power; he meets with disgrace. Continuing shame.

‹› 4. (9) No game in the field.

‹› 5. (6) Fidelity constantly made into a virtue is good fortune for a woman, but unhealthy in a man.

‹› 6. (6 at the top) Prolonged excitement brings misfortune.

TUN
33. WITHDRAWAL

TEXT: Withdrawal has success. Steadiness yields small advantages.

FIGURE: A mountain under the sky. The uncommon man keeps at a distance from mediocre people, doesn't show anger and remains dignified.

◇ LINES: 1. (6 at the bottom) He turns tail and runs—danger. No progress in any direction.

◇ 2. (6) He lashes it down with a yellow oxhide thong. No one can untie it.

◇ 3. (9) To retreat while hampered is difficult and dangerous. Those who maintain a retinue of men and women are fortunate.

◇ 4. (9) Prudent withdrawal by the exceptional man brings good fortune, but withdrawal by the average man is disaster.

◇ ◇ 5. (9) An admirable retreat by a steady hand brings good fortune.

◇ 6. (9 at the top) A graceful retirement. Everything is favorable.

Ta Chuang
34. Great Power

TEXT: Great Power. Earnestness is favorable.

FIGURE: Thunder in the sky. The uncommon man never steps outside the path of integrity.

‹› LINES: 1. (9 at the bottom) Power in the toes. Advancing now brings misfortune, without a doubt.

‹› 2. (9) Steadiness brings good fortune.

‹› 3. (9) The mediocre man uses brute strength, but the uncommon man restrains himself. To continue to act forcefully is dangerous. When a goat butts the hedge, its horns become entangled.

‹› ‹› 4. (9) Persistence brings good fortune, and guilt vanishes. The hedgerow is parted, and his horns are not entangled. Power is like the axle in a big cart.

‹› 5. (6) In easy circumstances, he loses a ram's strength, but doesn't regret it.

‹› 6. (6 at the top) A goat butts into a hedge, and it can't go backward or forward; nothing will get him out. Understanding the difficulty brings good fortune.

CHIN
35. ADVANCE

TEXT: Advance. The powerful prince is given many horses. In one day he is received at court three times.

FIGURE: Fire blazes up out of the earth. The uncommon man personally reflects the brilliance of excellence.

‹› LINES: 1. (6 at the bottom) Kept back from advancement. Persistence brings good fortune. If one is not trusted, he should maintain an openness, and no mistake will be made.

‹› 2. (6) Sorrowful advancement. Evenmindedness brings good fortune, which one gets from a grandmother.

‹› 3. (6) Everyone trusts him. Regret disappears.

‹› 4. (9) Going forward like a woodchuck. Continuing is dangerous.

‹› ‹› 5. (6) Sorrow disappears. Don't mind about winning or losing. Going forward brings good fortune, and everything can be turned to advantage.

‹› 6. (9 at the top) Advancing with horns lowered is only good for punishing one's own city. Danger, followed by good fortune. No fault. Persistence will bring regret.

TEXT: Eclipse. Steadiness in a difficult time is favorable.

FIGURE: Light hidden in the earth. In the midst of the people, the uncommon man masks his light, but still it shines.

◇ LINES: 1. (9 at the bottom) Light waning during flight; his wings droop. The exceptional man fasts for three days while traveling. He has a mission, but his host may gossip about him.

◇ ◇ 2. (6) An injury in the left thigh. He saves someone with a strong horse. Good fortune.

◇ 3. (9) Wounded while hunting in the south. The great leader is taken. Obsessive tenacity should be avoided.

◇ 4. (6) He penetrates the belly from the left side, and sees the heart darkened. He passes through the courtyard gate.

◇ ◇ 5. (6) Prince Chi's light was darkened at court. Steadiness is favorable.

◇ 6. (6 at the top) No light, only darkness. He once climbed up to heaven, but then he fell to earth.

CHIA JEN
37. THE FAMILY

TEXT: The Family. Earnestness by a man is favorable.

FIGURE: Fire rises into wind. The uncommon man's words have substance and his behavior is unvarying.

‹› LINES: 1. (9 at the bottom) Strictness within the family, sorrow disappears.

‹› ‹› 2. (6) She doesn't finish anything. First and foremost, she must prepare food. Constancy brings good fortune.

‹› 3. (9) When family members are sharp with each other, severity brings regrets; the difficult situation leads to good fortune. If man and child grin and chatter, misfortune comes.

‹› 4. (6) She enriches the household. Great good fortune.

‹› ‹› 5. (9) The ruler's influence affects the family. Don't worry. Good fortune.

‹› 6. (9 at the top) His confidence earns him respect. At last, good fortune.

K'UEI
38. CONTRARIES

TEXT: Contraries. Good fortune in small matters.

FIGURE: Fire above a lake. Among his associates the uncommon man is singular.

⟨⟩ LINES: 1. (9 at the bottom) Sorrow vanishes. If your horses stray, don't chase them; they'll come back on their own. You see bad people, and don't make mistakes.

⟨⟩ ⟨⟩ 2. (9) He meets his lord in a narrow lane. No fault.

⟨⟩ 3. (6) He sees his wagon dragged back, his oxen beaten, his head shaved and his nose cut off. Nothing good at the start, but ending well.

⟨⟩ 4. (9) Alone in the midst of contraries. He meets a good man and mutual respect develops. Difficulties, but no mistake.

⟨⟩ ⟨⟩ 5. (6) Sorrow vanishes. his close relation bites through the skin. If he proceeds, how can he be mistaken?

⟨⟩ 6. (9 at the top) Alone in the midst of contraries. He sees a hog wallowing in mud and a wagonload of ghosts. At first he draws his bow in defense, but then he hesitates, and sets it aside, for the intended target isn't a robber, he's an in-law. As he goes ahead, it rains; good fortune.

CHIEN
39. OBSTRUCTED

TEXT: Obstructed. South and West is favorable. North and East is unfavorable. Seeing the great man is advantageous. Steadiness brings good fortune.

FIGURE: Water on a mountain. The exceptional man turns inwardly to cultivate his character.

◇ LINES: 1. (6 at the bottom) Going forward is obstructed, coming back is praised.

◇ 2. (6) The ruler's agent meets one obstacle after another, through no fault of his own.

◇ 3. (9) To go on leads to obstacles; he must come back.

◇ 4. (6) Going ahead leads to obstruction; staying put allows connections.

◇ ◇ 5. (9) When one is in severe trouble, friends come.

◇ 6. (6 at the top) Going ahead leads to obstruction, coming back has good fortune. Seeing the great man is advantageous.

TEXT: Letting go. South and West is favorable. When one has nothing to gain by going ahead, returning brings good fortune. When one has a lot to gain by advancing, then hustle brings good fortune.

FIGURE: Thunder and rain let loose. The exceptional man pardons crimes and forgives mistakes.

◊ LINES: 1. (6 at the bottom) No mistake.

◊ ◊ 2. (9) He kills three foxes in the hunt, and earns a golden arrow. Steadiness brings good fortune.

◊ 3. (6) If a man carries a load on his back, but then rides in a carriage, he draws the attention of robbers. To keep on leads to misfortune.

   • *The Master says*: Carrying a burden on the back is the business of a common man; a carriage is the appurtenance of a man of rank. Now, when a common man uses the appurtenance of a man of rank, robbers plot to take it away from him. If a man is insolent to those above him and hard toward those below him, robbers plot to attack him. Carelessness in guarding things tempts thieves to steal. Sumptuous ornaments worn by a young woman are an enticement to rob her of her virtue.

◊ 4. (9) Let go with your thumb. A friend will come that you can trust.

◊ ◊ 5. (6) The uncommon man lets go; good fortune. Average people show confidence in him.

◊ 6. (6 at the top) The prince shoots a hawk perched on a high wall. Everything is favorable.

• *The Master says:* The hawk is the object of the hunt; bow and arrow are the tools and means. The hunter is the man (who must make proper use of the means to his end). The exceptional man contains the means in his own person. He bides his time and then acts. Why then should not everything go well? He acts and is free. Therefore all he has to do is to go forth, and he takes his quarry. This is how a man fares who acts after he has made ready the means.

41. DWINDLING

TEXT: Dwindling with sincerity brings about great good fortune, and no blame. Persistence. To have a purpose is favorable. How might one show this? Even two small bowls are enough for an offering.

FIGURE: A lake at the foot of the mountain. The exceptional man controls his anger and curbs his appetite.

‹› LINES: 1. (9 at the bottom) Leaving quickly when work is done is not a fault, but consider how it might affect the work.

‹› 2. (9) Steadiness is favorable, but initiating anything would bring misfortune. He can help others increase without lessening his own portion.

‹› 3. (6) When three people travel together, one is lost. When one man travels alone, he finds a friend.

• *The Master says*: Heaven and earth come together, and all things take shape and find form. Male and female mix their seed, and all creatures take shape and are born.

‹› 4. (6) When a man diminishes his problems, he hastens the coming of happiness, and no mistake.

‹› ‹› 5. (6) Someone who won't take no for an answer gives him twenty tortoise shells for foretelling. Great good fortune.

‹› 6. (9 at the top) To gain without depriving others is not a mistake. Steadiness brings good fortune. Any movement is favorable. He finds followers, but no home.

I
42. GAIN

TEXT: Gain. He gains by starting something new. Crossing the big water is favorable.

FIGURE: Wind and thunder. If the exceptional man sees good, he copies it; if he sees evil, he corrects it.

‹› LINES: 1. (9 at the bottom) The time is propitious for major changes. Great good fortune. No error.

‹› ‹› 2. (6) Someone who can't be refused gives him twenty tortoise shells for divination. Sure steadiness brings good fortune. The ruler offers some tortoise shells to God. Good fortune.

‹› 3. (6) He gains through calamitous events. He isn't to blame if he is sincere and acts moderately. He presents his emblem of office to the prince.

‹› 4. (6) He acts in moderation and his advice to the prince is followed. He can profitably be employed when moving the capital.

‹› ‹› 5. (9) He is confident and benevolent, without question. Great good fortune. Truly, his kindness will be recognized.

‹› 6. (9 at the top) He doesn't benefit anyone, and someone hits him. His heart is unsteady. Misfortune.

• *The Master says*: The uncommon man calms himself before moving; he gathers his thoughts before speaking; he solidifies his relations before asking for something. By taking care of these three matters, the uncommon man's peace of mind is complete. But if a man tries to direct others when he himself is restless, they won't cooperate. If he is hesitant in his words, they won't rouse others. If he requests something without any prior relationship, it won't be done. Then, when no one agrees with him, those who would harm him draw near.

TEXT: Decisiveness. He decisively proclaims the truth of the matter at the royal court. Danger. He must inform the people of his own city that they may not bear arms. The advantage is in clearly defining a goal.

FIGURE: A lake sucked up to the sky. The exceptional man distributes bonuses to those working for him, but, being virtuous, accepts none for himself.

‹› LINES: 1. (9 at the bottom) Advancing in strength on his toes. He goes but doesn't succeed; it is his fault.

‹› 2. (9) He cries out in fear; gunshots echo in the night. Nothing to fear.

‹› 3. (9) Clenched jaws brings misfortune. The exceptional man is unwavering in his resolve; he walks alone and when he's caught in the rain, he gets muddy. People gossip, but no mistake has been made.

‹› 4. (9) His buttocks have been flayed, and he walks with difficulty. If he let himself be led around like a sheep, his grief would vanish. He hears these words but doesn't believe them.

‹› ‹› 5. (9) Weeds must be uprooted without hesitation. His moderation allows no mistake.

‹› 6. (6 at the top) No one to call on. Misfortune comes at the end.

Kou
44. Intercourse

TEXT: Intercourse. The young man is powerful. Marriage for such a man is not recommended.

FIGURE: Wind blows close to earth. The ruler publishes his commands in every part of the world.

◊ LINES: 1. (6 at the bottom) The cart wheel is held by a metal brake. Steadiness brings good fortune. To initiate any course of action invites misfortune. Even a lean pig might make a commotion.

◊ ◊ 2. (9) A fish is in the creel, no mistake. But that's of no help to the guests.

◊ 3. (9) His buttocks have been flayed, and he walks with difficulty. Trouble, but no great mistake is made.

◊ 4. (9) No fish in the creel. This develops into an unfortunate situation.

◊ ◊ 5. (9) Leaves of the crab apple tree drape over the melon, hiding its shape. Something falls out of the sky.

◊ 6. (9 at the top) He rubs horns in greeting; regret, but no mistake.

Ts'ui
45. Association

TEXT: Association with others means success. The ruler goes to his temple. Seeing the great man is favorable, and brings success. Steadiness is favorable. If great sacrifices are offered, good fortune will come. Any activity is favorable.

FIGURE: A lake above the earth. The exceptional man gathers up his weapons so that he can prepare for the unexpected.

‹› LINES: 1. (6 at the bottom) His sincerity does not last to the end, and people scatter and come together in confusion. He shouts, but then someone shakes his hand, and he laughs again. No reason to worry. He goes ahead without mistake.

‹› 2. (6) Being led into a situation will be profitable, with no fault. If he is totally sincere, even a small offering is looked on with favor.

‹› 3. (6) The gathering is sad; nothing helps. Going ahead is not a mistake, just a slight inconvenience.

‹› ‹› 4. (9) Great good fortune. No mistake.

‹› ‹› 5. (9) Because of his position, he can gather people together flawlessly. Some have no confidence in his work; he must maintain his virtue and steadfastness; then sorrow disappears.

‹› 6. (6 at the top) Sighing and weeping. No mistake.

SHENG
46. AMBITION

TEXT: Ambition has great success. One must see the great man to drive out worries. Going south brings good fortune.

FIGURE: Trees grow out of the earth. The uncommon man devoted to virtue begins by accumulating small things, and achieves something great.

‹› LINES: 1. (6 at the bottom) His advancement is welcomed. Great good fortune.

‹› 2. (9) With sincerity, bringing even a small offering is favorable. No mistake.

‹› 3. (9) He is promoted in an empty city.

‹› 4. (6) The ruler has him make offerings on Mount Ch'i. Good fortune, and no mistake.

‹› ‹› 5. (6) Steadiness brings good fortune. He climbs step by step.

‹› 6. (6 at the top) Climbing upward in the dark. Unwavering steadiness is favorable.

K'UN
47. LIMITATION

TEXT: Limitation has success and steadiness. The great man has good fortune with no mistake. He has something to say, but isn't believed.

FIGURE: A lake with no water. The exceptional man risks his life to carry out his will.

⟨⟩ LINES: 1. (6 at the bottom) Bare winter branches whip his buttocks as he enters a bleak valley. For three years he sees nobody.

⟨⟩ ⟨⟩ 2. (9) He reaches his limit eating and drinking. The prince with scarlet knee sashes is coming just now. Making an offering is favorable. To go ahead brings misfortune. No mistake.

⟨⟩ 3. (6) A man is faced by a stone wall, and leans into thorns and thistles. He goes inside his house but doesn't find his wife. Misfortune.

• *The Master says*: If a man permits himself to be oppressed by something that ought not to oppress him, his name will certainly be disgraced. If he leans on things upon which one cannot lean, his life will certainly be endangered. For him who is in disgrace and danger, the hour of death draws near; how can he then still see his wife?

⟨⟩ 4. (9) He comes very slowly, trapped in a golden carriage. Regret, but not for long.

◊ ◊ 5. (9) His nose and feet are cut off, because of difficulty with the minister with purple knee sashes. Joy comes quietly. To make offerings is advisable.

◊ 6. (6 at the top) He is entangled by creeping vines. He staggers, saying that he regrets coming this way. If he is sorry for this, and makes a new start, good fortune will come.

TEXT: The Well. A town may be moved, but not the well. Well water never dries up entirely nor overflows. Anyone coming or going may draw water from the well. If the rope is lowered almost all the way down to the water but the bucket breaks, that is unfortunate.

FIGURE: Water over wood. The exceptional man encourages the people with advice and helps them.

‹› LINES: 1. (6 at the bottom) Don't drink water from a muddy well or from an old well that animals avoid.

‹› 2. (9) Tadpoles dart at the well-hole. The water-pitcher is cracked and leaky.

‹› 3. (9) The well has been cleaned, but no one draws water from it. This makes my heart sad, for its water might be used. If the ruler is clear-headed, we all might enjoy good fortune.

‹› 4. (6) A well with well-laid tiling is not a mistake.

‹› ‹› 5. (9) The clear well water comes from a cold spring, good to drink.

‹› 6. (6 at the top) The well is never blocked, it is reliable. Great good fortune.

Ko
49. CHANGE

TEXT: Change. Once it is done, people believe it. Great success. Steadiness is favorable; sorrow disappears.

FIGURE: Fire rises out of a lake. The exceptional man schedules the year's work, and clearly defines the seasons.

‹› LINES: 1. (9 at the bottom) Securely wrapped in yellow oxhide.

‹› 2. (6) On the right day, a revolution may be accomplished. Going forward brings good fortune, with no mistake.

‹› 3. (9) Any action now is ill-advised, and continuing the present course is downright dangerous. When talk of revolution has been discussed three times, people start to believe it.

‹› 4. (9) Sorrow vanishes, and people have confidence in him. A change in government brings good fortune.

‹› ‹› 5. (9) The great man, like a tiger, changes. He is trusted even before the oracle is questioned.

‹› 6. (6 at the top) Like a leopard, the exceptional man changes, while the average man merely turns his face to a new loyalty. Going forward brings misfortune; stubbornly staying put brings good fortune.

Ting
50. Caldron

TEXT: Caldron. Great good fortune and success.

FIGURE: Fire on wood. The exceptional man establishes his destiny by being scrupulous in his position.

◇ LINES: 1. (6 at the bottom) The ting (three-legged ritual pot) is upturned, the better to remove decaying bits of meat. Living together unmarried for the sake of children is not a mistake.

◇ 2. (9) The ting is filled with food offerings. My rival envies me, but he can't hurt me, fortunately.

◇ 3. (9) The ting's handles are gone, so it is difficult to carry. Pheasant fat won't be eaten. Rain falls, sorrow is spent, and at last good fortune comes.

◇ 4. (9) The ting's leg breaks, and the meal intended for the ruler spills, soiling his clothes. Shame and bad luck.

• *The Master says:* His character is not equal to the office he occupies. Small virtue coupled with high situation, small wisdom with big plans, small strength with heavy burden—in these circumstances, he will seldom escape disaster.

◇ ◇ 5. (6) The ting has yellow handles with gold rings. Steadiness is favorable.

◇ ◇ 6. (9 at the top) The ting has jade rings. Great good fortune. Everything is favorable.

CHEN
51. THUNDERCLAP

TEXT: Thunderclap brings success. Loud thunder moves in, causing cries and nervous laughter. For a hundred miles around people are terrified, but no one lets the sacrificial spoon and cup fall.

FIGURE: Rumbling thunder. Even while shaking with fear, the exceptional man examines his life.

◇ LINES: 1. (9 at the bottom) Thunder frightens, but then laughter follows. Good fortune.

◇ 2. (6) Thunder brings danger. Reluctantly he lets go of his possessions and climbs nine hills. He shouldn't chase after the lost objects; in seven days he'll find them.

◇ 3. (6) Thunder startles and distracts. If this sparks some action, that's not a mistake.

◇ 4. (9) While it thunders, he gets stuck in the mud.

◇ 5. (6) Thunder comes and goes. Danger. Nothing may be lost, yet some matters must be taken care of.

◇ 6. (6 at the top) Thunder brings confusion; trembling people look on in terror. To go anywhere is inadvisable. If the chaos hasn't reached him, even though his neighbors are affected, then that's no mistake. his relatives gossip about him.

KEN
52. RESTING

TEXT: Resting. By immobilizing his back, he is no longer aware of his body. He goes into the courtyard but doesn't see the people in it. This is not a mistake.

FIGURE: Twin peaks. The exceptional man considers matters that may extend beyond local circumstances.

◊ LINES: 1. (6 at the bottom) Calming the toes. No mistake. Constant steadiness is favorable.

◊ 2. (6) Calming the calves. He can't help his leader, which makes his heart sad.

◊ 3. (9) Quieting the hips and making the lower spine rigid is dangerous; this suffocates the heart.

◊ 4. (6) Stilling the torso is no mistake.

◊ 5. (6) Relaxing the jaw muscles. His words are crisp, and sorrow disappears.

◊ ◊ 6. (9 at the top) Total relaxation. Good fortune.

CHIEN
53. UNFOLDING

TEXT: Unfolding. The young man marries. Good fortune. Steadiness is favorable.

FIGURE: A tree on the mountain. The exceptional man lives in dignity and virtue, and cultivates morality among the people.

‹› LINES: 1. (6 at the bottom) Wild geese drift toward shore. The younger son is in danger, and is discussed. No mistake.

‹› ‹› 2. (6) Geese drift toward the rocks. Eating and drinking joyfully and peacefully. Good fortune.

‹› 3. (9) Geese circle slowly toward the plains. The man leaves and doesn't come back. The woman is pregnant but doesn't give birth. Misfortune. Defending against spoilers is favorable.

‹› 4. (6) Geese gradually descends toward the tree. They may find good perches. No mistake.

‹› ‹› 5. (9) Wild geese gradually approach the hill. The woman doesn't give birth for three years, but in the end nothing can prevent it. Good fortune.

‹› 6. (9 at the top) Geese circle up to the heights. Goose feathers are useful in ceremonial dances. Good fortune.

KUEI MEI
54. THE NUBILE WOMAN

TEXT: The Nubile Woman. Going forward is inadvisable. Nothing helps.

FIGURE: Thunder over a lake. The exceptional man is aware from the beginning of the temporary nature of his actions, even as he keeps his goal constantly in mind.

⟨⟩ LINES: 1. (9 at the bottom) The young man lives with a man. A lame man can still walk. Going ahead bring good fortune.

⟨⟩ 2. (9) A one-eyed person can still see. The steadiness of a hermit is favorable.

⟨⟩ 3. (6) The nubile woman who was a servant becomes a kept woman.

⟨⟩ 4. (9) The nubile man waits almost too long, but in time she has a late marriage.

⟨⟩ ⟨⟩ 5. (6) When Emperor Yi married off his younger daughter, the princess's dress was not as beautiful as that of her bridesmaid. It's almost full moon. Good fortune.

⟨⟩ 6. (6 at the top) A man holds a basket with nothing in it. The man stabs a sheep, and no blood flows. Nothing does any good.

FENG
55. ABUNDANCE

TEXT: Abundance has success. When the ruler brings abundance, don't be sad, be like the noonday sun.

FIGURE: Thunder and lightning. The exceptional man decides lawsuits and levies penalties.

‹› LINES: 1. (9 at the bottom) When a leader meets his equal, ten days together is not a mistake. Going ahead is approved.

‹› 2. (6) The curtain is so heavy that the Big Dipper can be seen at noon. If he goes, he is not trusted and disliked. But if his confidence is built up, good fortune comes.

‹› 3. (9) The banner screen is so thick that small stars can be seen at noon. He breaks his right arm. No mistake.

‹› 4. (9) The tent fabric is so thick that the Big Dipper can be seen at noon. He meets a leader of equal standing. Good fortune.

‹› ‹› 5. (6) A variety of brilliant persons come around, congratulations are offered, and fame draws near. Good fortune.

‹› 6. (6 at the top) Abundance in his house. He protects his family, but when he looks out his gate, he doesn't see anyone. For three years he sees nothing. Misfortune.

Lu
56. The Stranger

TEXT: The Stranger has small successes. Steadiness brings good fortune to the traveler.

FIGURE: Fire on a mountain. The exceptional man is clear-headed and cautious in declaring judgments, and doesn't delay lawsuits.

‹› LINES: 1. (6 at the bottom) If the stranger trifles away his time, he invites his own misfortune.

‹› 2. (6) The traveler arrives at an inn carrying his valuables on his person. He wins the loyalty of a young servant.

‹› 3. (9) The inn where the traveler was staying burns down. He loses the trust of his young servant. To persist leads to danger.

‹› 4. (9) The traveler stays in a shelter, where he gets expense money and an ax. He laments that his heart is uneasy.

‹› ‹› 5. (6) He shoots a pheasant, but loses the arrow. In the end he wins praise and is offered a position.

‹› 6. (9 at the top) A bird burns its own nest. At first the stranger laughs, but then he cries aloud. By his carelessness he loses an ox. Misfortune.

SUN
57. COLD WIND

TEXT: Cold Wind succeeds in small matters. Seek advantage in a goal and in seeing the great man.

FIGURE: Penetrating Wind. The exceptional man carries on his business in the light of heaven.

‹› LINES: 1. (6 at the bottom) Advancing, retreating. The steadiness of a soldier is favorable.

‹› 2. (9) Wind sweeps under the bed. He hires a great many fortunetellers and psychic researchers. Good fortune. No mistake.

‹› 3. (9) Repeated stabbings. Sorrow.

‹› 4. (6) Sorrow vanishes. While hunting, he catches three kinds of animals.

‹› ‹› 5. (9) Steadiness brings good fortune. Sorrow vanishes. Everything is favorable. It was no way to begin, but there's a good ending. A warning three days before a change, a reconsideration three days after the change. Good fortune.

‹› 6. (9 at the top) Wind under the bed. He loses his money and his ax. Persistence brings misfortune.

Tui
58. Smugness

TEXT: Smugness means success. Steadiness is favorable.

FIGURE: Twin lakes. The exceptional man joins his friends for good talk and exercise.

‹› LINES: 1. (9 at the bottom) Complacency. Good fortune.

‹› ‹› 2. (9) Sincere happiness. Good fortune. Sorrow disappears.

‹› 3. (6) Gathering hedonistic pleasures. Misfortune.

‹› 4. (9) Calculated happiness is restless. He is ill but not dangerously, and finds joy.

‹› ‹› 5. (9) Trust in disruptive influences is dangerous.

‹› 6. (6 at the top) Seductive pleasures.

HUAN
59. ALIENATION

TEXT: Alienation has success. The ruler goes to his temple. Crossing the big water is advantageous. Steadiness is favorable.

FIGURE: Wind blows across water. The old rulers built temples for sacrifices to the Lord.

◇ LINES: 1. (6 at the bottom) He helps with a strong horse. Good fortune.

◇ 2. (9) When things fall apart, he hurries to his private refuge. Sorrow disappears.

◇ 3. (6) He has no regard for himself. No sorrow.

◇ 4. (6) He disbands his old group. Great good fortune. The scattering leads in turn to gathering new talent, not something that ordinary men would think of.

◇ ◇ 5. (9) With flying perspiration, he makes his proclamation. He distributes the stores in the granaries. No mistake.

◇ 6. (9 at the top) His blood scatters. He keeps fear at a distance and goes out. No mistake.

60. REGULATION

TEXT: Regulation has success. If restrictions are heavy, they must not become permanent.

FIGURE: Dammed water above a lake. The exceptional man establishes guidelines and procedures for the exercise of correct conduct.

‹› LINES: 1. (9 at the bottom) He doesn't go past the door of his courtyard. No mistake.

• *The Master says*: Where disorder has arisen, words were the first steps toward it. If the ruler isn't discreet, he loses his minister. If the minister can't keep a secret, he loses his life. If things are not handled with discretion in the very beginning, their completion will be faulty. Therefore the exceptional man is careful to keep secrets, and does not speak.

‹› 2. (9) He doesn't go past the door of his courtyard. Misfortune.

‹› 3. (6) He doesn't seem to pay attention to the rules; he will have reason to lament. No mistake.

‹› 4. (6) Quietly limited. Success.

‹› ‹› 5. (9) Voluntary restriction brings good fortune. Advancing is respected.

‹› 6. (6 at the top) In severe restriction, stubbornness brings misfortune, then sorrow disappears.

CHUNG FU
61. AUTHENTICITY

TEXT: Inner peace affects even pigs and fish. Good fortune. Crossing the big water is advantageous. Steadiness is favorable.

FIGURE: Wind blows across a lake. The exceptional man carefully weighs the facts, and is not quick to sentence someone to death.

⟨⟩ LINES: 1. (9 at the bottom) He is self-confident; good fortune. To seek confidence elsewhere never brings peace.

⟨⟩ 2. (9) A crane calls out from her hiding place; her young ones answer. I have a fine full cup; come, share it with me.

• *The Master says*: The exceptional man stays in his apartment, and sends out his words. If they are well spoken, people will respond from a thousand miles away. How much more then from nearby! He stays in his apartment, and sends out his words; if they are not well spoken, opposition will arise a thousand miles away. How much more then from near by! Words come out of one's person and influence humans. Deeds are done close at hand and their effects can be seen far away. Words and actions are the hinge and bowspring of the exceptional man. As hinge and bowspring move, they bring honor or disgrace. his words and actions move heaven and earth. Can he then be careless?

‹› 3. (6) He meets his rival. Now he beats a drum, now he stops. He sobs, then he sings.

‹› 4. (6) Almost full moon. One of the pair of horses has wandered off. No mistake.

‹› ‹› 5. (9) He is completely self-assured, which joins others to him. No mistake.

‹› 6. (9 at the top) Cockadoodle-doo to the sky. Persistence brings misfortune.

Hsiao Kuo
62. Small Excesses

TEXT: Small excesses has success. Steadiness is favorable. Small things can be accomplished, but not large ones. The song of a bird flying tells us: Coming down is easier than striving upward. Great good fortune.

FIGURE: Thunder over a mountain. The exceptional man emphasizes reverence in his actions, sorrow in his bereavement, thrift in his expenditures.

◇ LINES: 1. (6 at the bottom) The flying bird meets with misfortune.

◇ ◇ 2. (6) He bypasses his grandfather to meet his grandmother. He doesn't reach the prince, but instead meets with his minister. No mistake.

◇ 3. (9) He takes no special precautions; somebody may stab him in the back. Misfortune.

◇ 4. (9) It's no mistake for him to confront the other, and not just pass him by. Proceeding brings danger, against which he must be on guard. He should not act, but remain unwavering.

◇ ◇ 5. (6) Dense clouds but no rain in the west. The prince shoots an arrow, hitting a bird in a cave.

◇ 6. (6 at the top) He sees him, but passes by, and doesn't greet him. The bird flies very high, unfortunately. Calamity and self-inflicted injury.

TEXT: All done. Small successes. Steadiness is favorable. Good fortune in the beginning, but in the end there will be disorder.

FIGURE: Water above fire. The exceptional man handles misfortune thoughtfully, having prepared himself for it ahead of time.

◊ LINES: 1. (9 at the bottom) He puts on the brakes; the back end gets wet. No mistake.

◊ ◊ 2. (6) The man loses her carriage-window curtain. She shouldn't chase after it, she'll get it back within seven days.

◊ 3. (9) The Illustrious Ancestor Wu Ting besieged the Devil's Country for three years before he conquered it. Mediocre people won't do for that kind of job.

◊ 4. (6) Even fine silk clothes turn to rags. Be on your guard all day long.

◊ 5. (9) The eastern neighbor sacrifices an ox, but that doesn't match his western neighbor's sincerity in offering a small spring ritual.

◊ 6. (6 at the top) His head is immersed in the water. Danger.

WEI CHI
64. UNREADY

TEXT: Unready. Success. The young fox is nearly across, but then he gets his tail wet. Nothing will help.

FIGURE: Fire above water. The exceptional man carefully differentiates things, in order to put each in its proper place.

‹› LINES: 1. (6 at the bottom) He gets his tail wet. Disgrace.

‹› 2. (9) He applies the brakes. Steadiness brings good fortune.

‹› 3. (6) Preparations are incomplete; to attack would bring misfortune. Crossing the big water is advantageous.

‹› 4. (9) Steadiness brings good fortune, and the disappearance of sorrow. Great effort was required to conquer the Devil's Country, but after three years, large territories were awarded.

‹› ‹› 5. (6) Steadiness brings good fortune. No sorrow. The brilliance of the exceptional man wins confidence. Good fortune.

‹› 6. (9 at the top) He drinks wine in total confidence of no error. But if his head gets foggy, he loses people's trust.